Is Your Relationship Castle Under Siege?

*31 Relationship Building Blocks
For A Happy Ending!*

Debbie Gerber

This book is written from the author's life experiences. This is not meant to be professional advice. The information is not for diagnosis or treatment. This information should not replace the help of a professional. If professional advice is required the services of a professional person should be obtained. The author is in no way responsible for or liable for the use of this material.

Printed in the United States

"My life is made up of memories

wherein my spouse

plays the starring role."

To my darling husband... thank you for your help, support, and participation in building a truly wonderful relationship castle. We have gone from a twitterpated, want to be together all the time, get a room relationship through the rocky road, stub our toes, cracking walls relationship to a stronger deeper twitterpated, wanting to be together all the time, get a room, committed to a happily ever after relationship. Thank you for the flowers that brighten my life. You are my hero. You are my best friend, the love of my life and my soul mate.

Table of Contents

IV - Ten More Blocks To Fortify Your Relationship Castle

V - Add Another Ten (Plus One Bonus) To Finish

VI - Final Thoughts

Introduction

According to fairy tales like Cinderella and the Hollywood movies, relationships are simple. All you have to do is find someone, fall in love, and live happily ever after. That's it, nothing more. It's no wonder then that so many women and men reach adulthood not truly knowing or understanding what it takes to keep a relationship strong and healthy.

Falling in love is easy; staying in love and growing together over time can be hard. It's not impossible though, and in fact it is easier than you might think... if you know and understand what it takes to keep a relationship vibrant and healthy.

WHAT DO A CASTLE AND A RELATIONSHIP HAVE IN COMMON?

Before a castle is built a person has a vision of what they want, expect and need. Once a plan has been made, reviewed revised and approved supplies are gathered and brought to the place where the castle is to be built and stand forever. The owner carefully follows the building of the castle and ensures that the plan is followed and construction stays on track. He makes sure that all the proper materials are used and that it is being constructed the way that the plans were drawn up. When necessary the builder makes changes so that the castle turns out to meet his expectations and needs. He makes sure that the castle is strong, able to withstand the elements and attacks from intruders.

When the castle is first built it looks perfect but it can quickly fall into disrepair through negligence. Castles need constant repair and upkeep. If repairs aren't quickly made as they occur the castle will start falling apart. The longer the upkeep is ignored and neglected, the more time and effort it takes to return the castle to like-new condition.

A relationship castle is built in a similar way. You find the person that meets your vision of what you want in a marriage partner. Then you make plans together for the future. You cement your unification as a couple by getting married. When you are first married your relationship seems perfect. Shortly thereafter little issues, annoyances, disagreements, and disappointments start to creep in. If you repair them as they occur your relationship castle will stay in pristine condition. If you take longer and ignore the problems they will grow into large cracks. These become harder and take longer to fix. Neglect your relationship too long and it will crumble.

Don't wait until divorce papers are produced to wake up and realize you want to save your relationship.

By that time the castle walls will have crumbled or been knocked down.

And that's why I wrote this book. This book is all about helping you to improve your relationship and keep it healthy. It doesn't matter if you're only vaguely dissatisfied, very unhappy, or at the end of your rope; everything contained inside this book can be used to help repair your relationship. It won't happen overnight, and there will be bumps along the way. The most important thing is to be willing to put in the necessary time and effort.

Why? Because there's no other way to put it – healthy and vibrant relationships take time and effort. Think of your relationship as a life long journey, not just a quick weekend trip. It's not enough to say "I love you" every once in a while and think everything will be just fine. You must be truly vigilant in your efforts, constantly striving to build up and improve yourself and your relationship.

...healthy and vibrant relationships take time and effort.

Based on my own research and experience I have found that relationships will get solid and stay that way when partners are proactive about nurturing it rather than letting the relationship just chug right along on cruise control. What most couples lack is not the desire to improve their relationship, but rather the knowledge and specific tools they need to achieve their desired result.

In our modern world relationships have become

"replaceable" and people are willing to throw them away at the first sign of trouble. When problems arise you should use the alternatives to giving up and letting go. Why? Because giving up and letting go is not the answer to your problems and it will not somehow allow you to move on to another, better relationship in the future. If you do not understand how to keep a relationship strong through good times and bad, then no relationship you have will ever become deep, connected, and fulfilling to your heart and soul.

GETTING THE MOST FROM THIS BOOK

I have provided you with the clear, straightforward, and easy to understand information you need to make your relationship a priority and make your castle strong. The ideas I present here are all from the "real world" and really do work; all you have to do is put them into action. You do not, however, have to put them into action all at once or in any particular order. That's the power and the beauty of what you'll find here; the information is flexible, customizable, and focused specifically on giving you the tools necessary to improve your relationship even beyond what you ever thought possible.

I have chosen to use the word relationship instead of marriage. Envision your emotional connections from an internal personal perspective. I also chose to use the term partner rather than spouse to get you to think of your marriage as a unified balanced partnership.

The way to get the most effective results from this book is to read it through completely, taking notes along the way especially when you read things that apply to your relationship or strike you as something you need to work on. Once you have finished take a look at your notes. Go back through the book to the parts where you found ideas or suggestions of interest. Re-read the ones you think are the best fit for your situation, and make plans for applying what you have learned.

It's also a good idea to formulate a "plan" in your own mind of what you want to accomplish, which steps you think will work best to help you achieve your goals, and how you will know when you have actually achieved them. This plan should not be harsh or inflexible; rather, it should allow for you to make adjustments and adapt as needed along the way so that you achieve the end result you set out to accomplish.

Finally, keep this book handy and refer back to it regularly. No matter how great your relationship might be, it will need constant effort and proactive attention to stay that way. The information in this book is specially designed to make it simple to keep your relationship running strong and healthy.

Please Note: If you're involved in a relationship that is abusive, the information in this book can help if both you and your partner are willing to work on strengthening the relationship and making it healthy. Nevertheless, I strongly suggest you also seek guidance, insight, or even professional help from someone who has experience in this area.

Nobody should have to live with any form of abuse, whether it is emotional, physical, or otherwise. You deserve to live a wonderful, fulfilling, and happy life (even if you don't think so at the moment), so seek out whatever you need to stand up for yourself and insist on a healthy, abuse-free relationship. You will be amazed at just how much stronger and happier you feel!

Are you ready to begin creating the relationship you truly want? That's great; let's get going right away!

Relationship Refresher

Everyone knows a healthy relationship is really important, but how many of us truly know what a healthy relationship looks and feels like? Simple as this may sound, a startling number of people have only the vaguest idea of what makes a relationship healthy, or worse, they have totally misguided and misinformed ideas about what makes a relationship healthy.

Before moving on to the real heart and soul of this book, let's get to a basic definition and understanding of what makes a relationship healthy.

WHAT IS A HEALTHY RELATIONSHIP?

A truly healthy relationship can be described with the following words:

- Committed
- Grateful
- Kind
- Honest

- Non-threatening
- Tolerant
- Supportive
- Devoted

- Aware
- Unified
- Patient
- Trusting

- Respectful
- Interested
- Concerned
- Sharing

In its very best and most noble moments, a healthy relationship is nothing short of magical.

An unhealthy and/or unhappy relationship, on the other hand, can also be easily described. Some of the most common words you might use include the following:

- Selfish
- Defensive
- Mean
- Unkind
- Revengeful
- Rude
- Jealous
- Insensitive

- Impatient
- Ignorant
- Indifferent
- Destructive
- Manipulative
- Unequal
- Deceitful

Now, anybody who has ever been in a relationship for any length of time knows that any of the above terms – either positive or negative – can be a part of a relationship at some point in its existence. It's just human nature to be imperfect and this shows up clearly in relationships. Everyone's castle forms a few cracks now and then.

The great news, though, is that no relationship has to stay mired in a negative situation. You have the power to change it if you truly want to by putting in the time and effort necessary to do your part to be the best partner you can possibly be.

Everything here is focused on teaching you the basics of a strong relationship, such as patience, honesty, listening, communication, and much more. Read and re-read the material presented here and you will soon find yourself with a very clear and helpful understanding of what it means to have a healthy, vibrant and enriching relationship.

YOUR RELATIONSHIP IN THE REAL WORLD

That's just fine, you might say. It's all too easy to talk about what it takes to build and maintain a healthy relationship; what's hard is to put that information to good use in the real world.

Let's face it, our busy lives are full of distractions each and every day; from parenting responsibilities to the demands of a career to the simple annoyances of daily life, it is incredibly easy to become lost in our own "world" and forget about others, especially our partner.

It's sad how we will often spend time and energy focusing on these other things and yet will devote little or no time to what's the most important; our partner and our relationship. We take for granted that our partner will always be there no matter what, so it's okay to divert attention to something more pressing and immediate. In other words, when we do this our relationship is constantly pushed to the "back burner" of the priority list. It should come as no surprise that a relationship in this situation over time will grow stale, cold, and distant.

So how, exactly, can we focus on improving and strengthening our relationship when faced with so many other distractions and demands for our time and attention? The answer is simple:

– Start With Yourself! –

The most important thing to understand is that building a healthy relationship begins with you. That's right you! It's critical to take the first steps yourself, without expecting anything in return from your partner. In other words, be proactive; become the best partner you can be. Focus your best efforts and energy on doing everything necessary to be an engaged, interested, and committed partner.

Chances are that by taking this approach, your partner will notice something is different and begin responding in kind. He or she may not respond in exactly the way you want or expect, but that's okay; any response at all shows that you and your partner have taken the first small, shaky steps toward mending and strengthening your relationship. Even if your partner shows no response at all, that's okay too; you have still started the process in motion and can build from there.

> *...be proactive; become the best partner you can be...*

Regardless of whether your partner responds or not, the next step is to open, or re-open the lines of communication between the two of you. This is often the hardest part because it involves revealing your own thoughts, feelings, and frustrations while also listening to those same things from your partner. As difficult as it may be, it is important to get the lines of communication as open as possible to allow each of you to stand up for yourself, express what you want, ask for what you need, and explain why it's important.

Do you remember when you first learned to ride a bike? You probably started with training wheels and a trusted adult guiding you and encouraging you as you learned. Eventually you learned how to balance on your own, and the training wheels came off and best of all, once you have learned how to ride that bike you will never forget. Years and years may go by without riding, but all you have to do is get back on and ride. You'll probably be a little rusty at first, but you'll quickly shake that off in no time at all.

The same concept holds true for communicating with your partner. If you have never experienced solid communication, use the tools in this book to put on your relationship "training wheels" and work together to figure out what to do. If, however, you know what to do but have become rusty over the years then all you have to do is oil the chain, get "back on the bike" and get back into practice.

A REAL LIFE EXAMPLE

Let's look at a real life example of re-opening the lines of communication and asking for what you want in a relationship. I remember a few years ago when my own marriage was stuck on "auto pilot" and our life routine was so high stress that we had allowed it to drain our relationship of emotional interaction and fulfilment. I felt I had lost myself. I needed to know that my husband loved me for me and not for the business partner I had become. I had reached a point in my life where I desperately needed to spend more time focusing on those things that had been too often shoved aside or ignored. I felt a bit like a princess, trapped in the tower, unable to make my way out.

My husband and I needed to talk openly and honestly, and I had to be the one to initiate the discussion. Why? Because even though we had been married for many years, he simply did not understand what I needed or wanted. He knew that I was unhappy but he was busy and stressed and just assumed "no news was good news." I was reluctant to tell him what I needed. I thought, how could he not "just know" what I needed? Why did I have to tell him out loud when we had been together long enough that he should have instantly realized what had changed and understood why it was so important to me?

> *My husband and I needed to talk openly and honestly, and I had to be the one to initiate the discussion.*

Sometimes it was rough at first, but before long we were communicating more openly and clearly than we had in a very long time. It still took some time, though, for him to really understand, accept, and support what I was saying.

He tried hard to understand right from the start, but I was asking him to think in an entirely new way and consider something completely new in my life. It took a few talks for us to get "on the same page."

In the end, I realized he had always loved me for me and wanted me to be happy and fulfilled, but he didn't realize my wants and needs had evolved. He thought everything was just fine the way it was. I had to explain what I needed from him in a way that he could understand and support.

Don't forget this wasn't just about me. I found I had neglected things he needed from me as well. We both had to listen, accept and act to fulfill the needs and wants of the other person.

So why were we so successful in our discussion? What were the keys to communicating with each other effectively and clearly? Here are some of the "lessons learned" from my experience:

- *Share information kindly, patiently, calmly, and slowly*
- *Explain what you need several times and in several different ways*
- *Have several conversations on the same subject to let it sink in*
- *Ask specifically for what you want − don't*

hint!

- *Don't expect your partner to "just know" what you want*
- *Be direct; don't beat around the bush*
- *Don't pout, act like a baby, threaten, scream or attack*
- *Give the details necessary for your partner to understand*
- *Stand up for yourself, but don't be brutish, rude or aggressive*

If you follow these guidelines in your discussions, chances are you will enjoy the same kind of success, satisfaction, and relationship improvements I did. Even if it seems too difficult, be brave and stick with it – you'll be glad you did in the end!

THE "LIST" EXERCISE

Here's a great exercise to do with your partner as a way to keep the lines of communication open and ensure that you both understand what the other person wants and needs from the relationship. The results just might surprise you both, and will almost certainly be the starting point for really in-depth and meaningful discussions.

Step 1 – Make a list of what you want and need from your partner.

This might include things such as more affection; sharing decision making; letting you sleep in on the weekend; support in a career choice; who does the grocery shopping; or anything else that is important to you. It doesn't matter if these things are big or small, what's most important right now is to capture them and record them as part of your list.

Before adding an item to your list, review carefully what the outcome will be when you get what you are asking for. Is this really the thing that makes a big difference for you? When your list feels complete, review what you wrote and think about each item; narrow it down to the three most important things you truly want and need from your partner.

When you're finished with your own list, start a new list of what you think your partner wants and needs most from you. Again, focus on capturing your thoughts and getting them recorded on paper. When you've run out of items, review the list and narrow it down to the three things you think your partner needs most from you.

Your partner will follow this same process. First, identifying the three things he/she most wants and needs from you; then identifying the three things he/she thinks you most want and need. Be sure to set aside plenty of time for both of you to think about and finish your lists.

Step 2 – Share the lists with each other.

When you are both finished making lists, sit down in a quiet place that's free from distractions so you can share the lists with each other and discuss what you find. Both of you should agree in advance to some basic communication ground rules:

- *Listen without interrupting*
- *Ask questions in non-defensive tones*
- *Be patient, be kind, and be understanding of feelings*
- *Do not accuse, dismiss, attack, diminish, or otherwise tear them or their needs down*
- *Treat each other with love and respect*

Now you're ready to share your lists with each other. You can simply trade papers and read each other's lists or choose to read them out loud to each other. What matters the most is that you both share your lists in their entirety before your discussion begins.

Chances are you will find at least one, but more likely several, mismatches between what the two of you want from each other as well as what you each think the other person wants. Don't be discouraged if this is the case, because this is exactly the point and purpose of the exercise. It is through sharing individual needs, wants, dreams, and ideas and then identifying any misunderstandings that you can move forward with additional conversations that are necessary for resolving your differences and strengthening your relationship.

Be prepared for this initial conversation to be lengthy, and always adhere to the communication ground rules no matter how tempting it may be to dismiss or attack your partner. Most couples have many conversations over several days to focus in on issues that require more discussion to understand and resolve. Again, this is okay and is actually a very good thing because it allows each of you to practice communicating in a loving and respectful way.

Step 3 – Create an action plan for improvement.

The final step is to create an action plan. This does not have to be lengthy or complicated; in fact, the simpler it is the better. Why? Because if things get too complicated or complex you are very likely to fall back into old habits. Start with simple, straightforward steps that you can both agree on and stick to.

The action plan should be clear and specific enough that the two of you can follow it and refer back to it regularly to check your progress. The action plan should include at least the following:

- *Know what your partner needs from you*
- *Have a full understanding of why they want it*
- *Know how you can provide it*
- *Both partners acknowledge effort and offer encouragement when mistakes or missteps occur*
- *Agree on how you will acknowledge and celebrate when needs are fulfilled successfully*

Remember, the whole purpose of this exercise is for each partner to ask for what they want and then to successfully fulfill each other's needs, not to relegate your partner to languish in the dungeon.

Don't worry if you have a few missteps or even false starts along the way, because this is normal and to be expected. It will take some practice before you are able to go through this process smoothly.

Do you recall when we talked about "training wheels" a bit earlier in this chapter? The concept applies here as well; start with the small, easy steps so you can experience the benefits that come from having success. Having these small successes under your belt will build a strong castle foundation for taking on the more difficult issues that arise.

ANOTHER REAL LIFE EXAMPLE

Let's look at another of my real life examples, this time focusing on the list exercise. My husband and I did this exercise together, thinking that we would be pretty much "in sync" with each other because we had been married for a long time. Let me tell you, the results really surprised us. Even though we had been married for many years, our lists still didn't match. Neither of us correctly identified all of the other person's three most important wants and needs. Talk about a wake-up call!

I figured after years of marriage my husband should know me well enough to understand...

For instance, one of the things I need from him is to receive fresh flowers. It's a simple thing, really, but to me it is important because it makes me feel happy, wanted, and loved. I figured after years of marriage my husband should know me well enough to understand that this is one of my needs, even if it is a relatively small item. He should just "know" to bring me flowers periodically, right? Wrong!

I dropped hints like crazy, hoping he would catch my drift. "Did you know women like flowers?" I would say, "Don't you think some fresh flowers would look nice on our dining room table?" I would hint, but no luck. He just didn't "get it" that I wanted him to bring me flowers. Even when I was direct and said "You should bring me flowers" he still didn't seem to hear me or even care what I was saying. Needless to say, I grew resentful, angry, and just plain mad at him.

It's not like he didn't do many other really sweet things for me. He would bring home a funny card with a cute saying on it, or a cuddly stuffed animal, or even my favorite chocolate candy. To his credit, he thought he was doing things that would make me happy; after all, what wife wouldn't feel special if she received these kinds of gifts? But no, it wasn't what I really wanted so I continued feeling resentful despite his good intentions. I even got to the point where I would buy flowers for myself, just hoping he would get the hint.

SURPRISE, SURPRISE, SURPRISE!

You can imagine, then, his surprise when "bring me flowers" showed up in the top 3 of my list of wants and needs. He had been trying to please me, but it took doing the "list exercise" for him to realize what I truly wanted. His thinking is that flowers are a waste of money because they die quickly, and that you can just grow them in the yard and enjoy them there. As we talked about it, I told him just how important it is for me to receive flowers from him. They make me smile, and they create strong feelings of warmth and love toward him. He had a hard time understanding why I would want him to spend money on something that didn't last very long, but eventually I explained it in enough detail for him to "get it" and understand.

Next, we created an action plan for this list item. I helped him identify some places to buy flowers at a reasonable price in locations convenient for his work commute and shared with him a few of my favorite kinds of flowers. When he brought flowers home for me I thanked him and shared with him how much I enjoyed smelling them and how it made me smile and feel more loving toward him because he had been so thoughtful. I acknowledged his effort and before long it became a wonderful new habit that he enjoyed too, simply because it made him feel good seeing me smile and feeling so happy.

After working through the "List Exercise" things are much better. I now work on providing the things on his list for him and he brings me flowers and works on providing the other things on my list for me. As a result, I feel warm and happy, and we celebrate the improved strength and depth of our relationship that comes from expressing and fulfilling important wants and needs.

BUILD ON YOUR SUCCESS

Once you have successfully made it through the list exercise, it's tempting to think that everything is "fixed" and you're all done with the process. Do not give in to this temptation! Remember, just as the stone walls of a castle need to be repaired over time, wants and needs change over time as circumstances and life change. It's important to check in with each other regularly to ensure you continue to build on your initial success.

Set aside a time, at least monthly, to spend together reviewing each other's lists. Evaluate how you are doing on your action plan and make any changes or adjustments that might be necessary. Most couples find it really easy to delay this or let other things crowd their schedule so that there is no time left to have these discussions. Don't let this happen to you! Schedule your talking sessions as "must attend" meetings on your calendar, something that takes priority over all but the most extreme emergencies. As the months go by, your relationship will continue to grow stronger, closer, and more intimate.

It's important to go through the entire "list exercise" with each other every year. Start from scratch with your lists, following the complete process from start to finish. This is a terrific way to step back and take an overall look at wants and needs, evaluating any changes that have occurred in the previous twelve months. For most couples who are diligent about their monthly progress checks, the annual renewal is a chance to acknowledge past successes and build on them by expanding their understanding of each other's evolving wants and needs.

A FEW MORE TIPS TO CONSIDER

Most men are more comfortable having an in-depth conversation when sitting side by side rather than face to face. This may sound like a stereotype, but in general it is true. There are a number of reasons why this is the case, most of which are beyond the scope of this book. What's most important is to set your-selves up for success by ensuring your converstaion takes place in an environment where both partners are most willing to open up.

It's perfectly okay to have your discussions in the car, preferably parked in a quiet location rather than while driving when you need to concentrate on the road. You can also get out of the car and sit on a park bench, sit on the swings at the local playground, or take a walk along a nearby path. If you prefer to stay close to home, avoid sitting in the same old places you normally sit. Lie on a blanket in the backyard, sip some lemonade on the porch steps, sit in your lawn chairs at sunset, or languish in the hot tub.

The most important thing is to stay away from your normal routine, avoid external distractions, and have plenty of time so you don't have to hurry. You can't be in the middle of your discussion and have to quit because you are out of time. One way to solve this if you are pressed for time is to set up several smaller discussions close together. Set them up like you would any other important appointment. Set up a time and date an example would be to set aside every Tuesday, Wednesday and Friday from 8:30 p.m. to 9:30 p.m.

Select whatever days and times work best for you. It's also a good idea to keep some tissues handy, because chances are at some point the tears will flow and one (or both) of you will appreciate having them nearby.

When things get hard and you start to doubt yourselves, remember this: building a solid, loving, and healthy relationship takes time and commitment from both partners. It's common for partners to disagree during their conversation, that's alright as long as you are respectful of each other's feelings.

Sometimes it's best to agree to disagree for a while as you work through your issues.

Sometimes it's best to agree to disagree for a while as you work through your issues. Focus on understanding your partner's perspective and lovingly explain your perspective as well. If you are both committed to success and willing to open up with your vulnerabilities and emotions, with time and effort you can resolve disagreements so that both of you come out of it happier, stronger, and closer to each other. Soon you'll be sitting side by side on your thrones of a solid relationship.

TAKE THE RELATIONSHIP QUIZ

Before we move on to more ways to help strengthen and improve your relationship, let's pause for a few moments to assess the current state of your relationship. I have put together this quiz as a tool to help you identify aspects of your relationship that are in good shape, as well as aspects where attention and improvement are needed.

This quiz is simply a way to get you thinking. While taking this quiz you may identify some indicators that show that your relationship could use some attention or show areas where your relationship is strong.

Here are the quiz questions:

- Does your partner roll their eyes at you when you talk to them?
- Do they shake their head in derision while you are talking?"
- Do you often say to yourself or under your breath, "What a jerk?"
- Do you find that you say, "I hate you" whether to their face or to their retreating back?
- Are your thoughts when apart from each other all about how you can't wait to see your partner again?
- Do you text or call your partner during the day because you miss him or her?
- Do you often think, "How sweet of him/her?"
- Do you often think, "I just love him/her?"

- Is your description of him "My Hero?"
- Do you just love to spend time talking to your partner?
- Do conversations you have with your partner that touch on anything personal make you cry?
- Do you think, "Why bother even trying, he/she doesn't care anyway?"
- Do you think, "It doesn't matter what I think anyway?"
- Does your partner say, "The dog, kids, or hobby get more attention than I do."
- Have you thought, "Maybe he/she will just die and go away?"
- Have you ever thought, "Maybe if I were in an accident then he/she would be sorry I'm gone?"
- Do you have common goals?
- Do you miss him/her when you are apart?
- Are you attracted to your partner?
- Do you decide together how to handle your money?
- Do you call each other names when you are angry?
- Do you take time to be alone with each other, minus children or friends?
- Are you happy with your relationship?
- Do you find that you complain to your friends about your partner all the time?

- Do you feel your partner really knows you?

- Do you feel you are drifting apart?

- Do you have similar likes and dislikes?

- Do you feel you can express your feelings without being judged or condemned for them?

- Do you resent your partner?

- Do you know your partner's dreams, fears, things that make him/her happy, what he/she hopes to accomplish in life?

- Do you feel you can go to your partner when you are sad, hurt, unhappy, angry or when you need comfort, support or strength,?

- Do you feel life is better with your partner rather than without him/her?

- Do you look for or expect that your partner will wrong, hurt, or offend you?

After identifying strengths or weaknesses uncovered by the quiz questions read the following chapters to address these issues. Please note all of the ideas in this book can help every relationship.

Ten Building Blocks For A Strong Relationship Castle

Welcome to the heart and soul of this book – the relationship building blocks that can serve as important tools for reinforcing and strengthening your relationship castle. Each of these represents a particular approach to resolving the most common relationship issues while building up the strength and quality of your relationship.

While each idea presented here is different, they all have one thing in common – you and your partner are integral parts of achieving success. Regardless of how silly, scary, or strange the idea might seem, if you commit yourselves to following the process and actively engaging with each other, good results will soon emerge.

Are you ready to take off on an exciting relationship adventure? Great, here are the 31 Relationship Building Blocks.

YOUR PARTNER: MIP

Looking at successful relationships, one thing becomes apparent in every one of them: each person views their partner as being a "most important person" who is their primary life priority. This may seem incredibly obvious, but you would be surprised at just how many people do not put their partners first and treat them as a "most important person."

Even more interesting is that most of these same people think they are already doing this. In their minds, their partner already is first priority and so they don't see the need to make any changes. Why? Because they don't fully understand what it really means to put their partner first.

Treating your partner as the highest priority in your life can take a number of different forms...

Treating your partner as the highest priority in your life can range from the very simple to the more complex. Take a look at some examples of this approach in action:

- When your partner wants to say something or talk to you, give him/her your full attention. This means turning off the TV, turning down the radio, putting down the newspaper, and making focused eye contact.

- Hang up the phone and let calls go straight to voice mail when your partner is talking or needs you.

- If schedule conflicts arise, check with your partner before agreeing to any proposed changes.

- When your partner calls, stop what you are doing and politely excuse yourself to take the call. If an explanation is necessary tell them that the call is coming from your partner and that you need to answer it.

- Teach children that your partner is the first to receive attention when needed. They need to learn that their mom and dad require a few moments to focus on each other.

- Listen without interrupting. Only when your partner is finished talking should you ask questions, check for understanding, or ask for clarifications.

- If you do not understand something your partner says or does, respectfully ask them to explain in more detail. Repeat back what you heard them say to ensure both of you clearly understand each and are on the same page

Now, of course there will sometimes be circumstances where it's not appropriate to set everything else aside and focus on your partner such as when a dragon is chasing you around the courtyard, so to speak. Now that can't wait. The reality is, however, that dragons don't appear all that often. Extreme situations occur much more seldom than most people think. If you are truly committed to treating your partner as a "most important person" you will take action in a way that is polite, courteous, and respectful.

Debbie Gerber

APPRECIATE AND ACKNOWLEDGE

We all have the need to be appreciated and acknowledged for our contributions, so make a point of doing this with your partner. This is one of the hardest of all the building blocks to sustain long term. Why? Because it's all too easy to take your partner for granted, whether it's the little things he/she does or the larger contributions.

I am most likely to forget to show my appreciation to my husband when life becomes busy, stressful, or both. I sometimes take it for granted when he does the dishes, takes the dog for a walk, cleans up the house, or something similar. It seems the busier I get, the less I notice the things he does. It's a vicious circle that I must consciously choose to disrupt.

The key to consistently showing your appreciation and acknowledgement is to pay attention to your partner's actions, no matter how insignificant or small they may seem to you. Sometimes I literally have to force myself to pause for a moment and write down what happens to keep from forgetting or overlooking anything. Then, as soon as possible, I thank my husband and express my sincere gratitude for what he has done.

> *No matter how small, no matter how minor, I make sure he knows how much I appreciate him.*

No matter how small, no matter how minor, I make sure he knows how much I appreciate him. I know he appreciates the acknowledgement and gratitude

35

I offer and is thus more likely to continue doing the things that I appreciate. This cycle of action followed by gratitude is one that, once started, will continue to build upon itself and grow stronger with time.

GIVING WITHOUT EXPECTATIONS

Many couples fall into the unfortunate pattern of only giving of themselves or doing something for their partner if they expect to receive something in return. This is a pattern that occurs throughout life and the world around us. Very few people are willing to give up something of value unless they are assured of getting something of value back. It is this kind of selfishness – and that's truly what it is – that holds you back from creating a better and stronger relationship with your partner.

So why not try something different? Make a point of giving to your partner without any expectation of receiving anything in return. This can be something as simple as giving him/her a cup of coffee without being asked, or as big as setting aside one of your wants or desires in order to make his/her want or desire come true first.

When you give more to the relationship than you expect to get back, you are giving your partner the most precious and valuable gift possible – a piece of yourself. Giving without expectation or desire for something in return allows you to express your deepest love and devotion to your partner. This strengthens the exterior of your castle and lights a fire within its walls.

It also helps to directly ask your partner what he/she wants. Find out what makes them happy, what you can do to increase their happiness or comfort, and what they want from the relationship. Even when you have done the "List Experience" it is still a good idea to occasionally ask.

If you ask, though, you must be prepared to follow through and take the action(s) your partner will find meaningful. Even if it's difficult for you or it feels a bit strange, when you dive in and put yourself out there for your partner, the relationship becomes stronger and healthier.

IN SPITE OF THEMSELVES

 Most people, on some level, have doubts about their own self worth or value. Even the strongest and most confident person sometimes worries he/she is not strong enough, good enough, smart enough, etc. Many others are quite self-destructive, not believing in their own self worth or abilities.

How does this show up in your partner? You might hear them say:

- *I'm not lovable*
- *I'm not good enough or smart enough*
- *I'm not capable enough*

- *I'm not worthy of being loved*
- *You'd be better off without me*
- *I'll never get it right*
- *I'm so stupid or I'm such an idiot*
- *I'm a failure*
- *I'm fat or I'm ugly*

Even if your partner does not come right out and express these thoughts directly, chances are you can sense when they are lurking around causing them problems. It is at these times – when your partner feels weakest and most unlovable – that you must give your love openly, freely, and in large quantities. Strive to show your partner, through actions and words, how valuable and lovable he/she truly is.

If you hear them say negative, self-deprecating things about themselves, encourage them by letting them know that you don't agree with that. Give them a reason why you think that it isn't true, or expand on something positive about them. If they say, "I'm so stupid" you might say, "I don't think so ... you fixed the faucet? That isn't something I could have done or most other people could have done, unless they were a professional plumber. I think you are brilliant!"

In other words, love your partner wholeheartedly, despite what they think or say about themselves. This is real, true unconditional love that has the power to transcend everything and even make a relationship whole again. Go ahead and do it. You just might be surprised at how fulfilling and satisfying it is to give of yourself unconditionally in this way!

FORGIVE INSTANTLY

 Hang up your sword and take off that suit of armor, because forgiveness is perhaps the most powerful tool at your disposal for strengthening and improving your relationship. There is simply no substitute for offering your partner complete and immediate forgiveness. Most people will say they are willing to forgive their partner only after some time has passed and after their partner has been made very aware of their transgression. Even if they apologize they will forgive for a moment and then keep a little something on the side, just in case they need it later to use against their partner.

The problem with this approach is that it causes problems, issues, and hurts to linger far beyond the time that they should, creating a constant sense of dread that something awful is hanging right over their head just waiting to fall.

It takes a conscious choice on your part to forgive and move on...

Just as immediate complete forgiveness is extremely powerful; it can also be extremely difficult. It takes a conscious choice on your part to forgive and move on rather than let issues fester and create even bigger problems down the road. If you struggle with being able to truly offer forgiveness quickly, completely, and consistently, here are some ways to overcome this struggle:

- *Forgive every time; no exceptions, no excuses*
- *Don't bring up past faults, actions, or hurts. Once you have forgiven, the situation is over, period!*
- *Don't re-live past issues in your head, simply forgive and let it go.*
- *Give the benefit of the doubt every time*
- *Always assume the best about your partner*
- *Keep an open mind; consciously choose not to take offense*
- *Avoid dwelling on the past, and instead choose to embrace the future*
- *Don't retaliate, strike back, or otherwise try to get revenge*

Many times we prepare or set ourselves up to be hurt or offended in advance as we anticipate what our partner might or might not say. For instance, if he/she says "Are you going to wear that?" before heading out to dinner. Don't assume the real message is "It makes you look fat" or something similar. Instead, consider their words, their tone of voice, and their intent most of the time you will find that their intentions were completely innocent.

When you need to know what they meant, ask your partner for clarification in a respectful way...

Give them the benefit of the doubt. They may be thinking nothing more than you look so nice that they don't feel dressed up enough to match you.

When you need to know what they meant, ask your partner for clarification in a respectful way without making accusations or flinging insults.

Pre-programming yourself to feel automatically hurt or offended is one of the easiest bad habits to form. It creates a no win situation. When you recognize yourself falling into this habit, build a new habit by stopping, thinking, and choosing a more positive and constructive result.

The truth is when it is your habit to forgive instantly and completely, both you and your partner benefit. Your partner receives the gift of forgiveness and a fresh start, while you give yourself the gift of a light heart by eliminating the burden of lingering hurts and other mental baggage. Remember, forgiveness allows them to see their mistake and make changes in themselves to improve and be able to please you next time. It's astounding, really, just how much lighter and more free you will feel just by leaving behind the heaviness of carrying a grudge.

KISSING

 Think back to when you and your partner were first growing close. When you thought they were a prince or a princess - the touch of a hand, the sound of a voice, and a sweet, tender kiss seemed like heaven right here on earth. Over time, though, you may have gradually drifted away from the simple gestures, like a kiss or a hug that can so powerfully communicate your feelings for each other.

It happens to nearly everyone, unfortunately. A busy schedule, coming and going, taking care of children, careers and all of the other responsibilities the two of you have can easily distract you from maintaining the simple ritual of kissing. The truth is that this very simple and easy gesture – kissing – is one of the most powerful tools for strengthening and improving your relationship. It's quick, it's easy, and it communicates volumes about your feelings for each other.

If you have fallen out of the habit of kissing, it's high time for you and your partner to fall back into this powerful ritual. Make a conscious choice to always kiss hello and kiss goodbye. If you find yourself out the door having forgotten to kiss, go back inside and correct the situation. This may sound a bit silly, but think about it for a moment. What could be more powerful and appreciated than if you stopped everything and went back for a kiss? The message to your partner is that he/she is the most important priority in your life, so much so that you're willing to "go the extra mile" to share that all-important kiss.

The simple act of kissing has tremendous value in the expression of affection.

The simple act of kissing has tremendous value in the expression of affection. A kiss can show love and forgiveness after a disagreement, comfort a broken heart, offer encouragement when the world seems to be falling apart, protect an ego and much, much more. Just as importantly, choosing to kiss each other regularly creates precious physical contact throughout the day rather than just at night when you go to bed. This is especially important when partners begin to feel the only time they are loved is when sex is desired.

Try a 15 second kiss it's more challenging, but comes with even greater rewards. If you and your partner really want to improve the relationship, commit to at least one kiss each day that lasts a minimum of 15 seconds. That's right, a 15 second kiss. The power of this type of kiss is in the instant connection it creates and the extended time during which that connection is maintained. You might be able to "fake" a quick kiss hello or goodbye, but it's hard to hide from the intense feelings and profound closeness generated by a simple extended kiss.

20 GIFT & NOTE IDEAS

A terrific way to express your love and strengthen your relationship castle is to do little favors, give little gifts, or leave little notes for each other. Even if your partner doesn't do these things for you, by doing it for them you clearly communicate love and create a feeling within them of stronger love for you. In other words, your partner feels special, loved, and appreciated, which is a critical part of every healthy relationship.

Why is this so powerful? Quite simply, because it shows that you are willing to put in the extra time and effort necessary to express your love so that your partner will feel warm and happy. I'm not talking about spending a lot of time and money or writing lengthy love poems; rather, I'm talking about doing little things that are easy and inexpensive yet speak volumes about how much you value your partner.

I've collected some examples taken straight from the real world of my own marriage. Each of these little acts of love I have done for my husband or he has done for me, and believe me, they mean a lot. Take a look:

- Give your partner a small stuffed animal holding a rose

- Leave a note on the bathroom mirror that says, "Good morning sexy"

- Leave little notes that say "I love you" in various places where your partner will find them and be surprised (under a pillow, in a briefcase, in a lunch box, in the underwear drawer, etc.)

- Leave a baggie of cinnamon bears under the windshield wiper of your partner's car while he/she is at work; include a note saying "I'm hot for you" and sign it with your name

- Write a letter listing all of the reasons why you love and admire your partner, then put the letter in the mail to be delivered in the regular mail

- Pick up your partner's favorite candy bar, cookies, or other sweet treat and put it on his/her pillow with a note saying "I love you," "Sweet dreams for a sweet person," "Nothing is as sweet as you" or something similar

- Send a quick text message like, "I think you're amazing," "I love you," "Can't wait to see you," or "I miss you"

- Change the screen saver on your partner's computer to a picture of you or of the two of you together

- Frame a favorite picture and put it on your partner's desk or in their work area

- In winter when it's cold, dark, and gloomy, bring home a daffodil or tulip with a note that says "You really put a spring in my step"

- Leave a note on the bathroom mirror using soap or a dry erase marker

- When you see a comic strip that reminds you of something about your relationship or your partner, cut it out and post it on the refrigerator

- Bring home a pizza, spread a blanket on the floor, and have a candlelight "picnic" in the living room

- Give your partner a back massage, complete with scented massage oil and soft music

- Deliver flowers to your partner while he/she is at work, at school, in exercise class, or the like

- Make a yard sign out of poster board that says "I love ...." and put it in the front yard

- Put an "I love you" stick-on tattoo in a place that only your partner will get to see

- Rent your partner's favorite movie, even if

it's one that you don't particularly like

- When the bathroom mirror, a car window, or something similar is steamed up, write, "I love you" on it; the next time it steams up again, your note will reappear

- Pick one of your partner's least favorite chores and do it for him/her

The list of things you could do for your partner is practically endless; it is only limited by your own imagination and creativity. Why not brainstorm a few ideas of your own? Or, keep a small notebook with you and jot down ideas when they occur to you.

Important: The key to success with this concept is to do it for fun, without expecting anything from your partner in return; it should truly be an unconditional gift of love from you. However, if your partner does choose to do things like this for you, by all means express your appreciation and count yourself as a very lucky person to have such a thoughtful partner!

WHAT ARE YOUR STRENGTHS?

Every partnership is just that, a partnership. It is not all about you or all about your partner. A partnership is a joining of your desires, strengths, and souls, into a castle fortress that can withstand anything. If your relationship is struggling or somehow feels out of balance, try doing an inventory of the strengths you each have to offer. Be honest with yourself and with your partner. Be careful that you identify only those things that are true instead of those you wish were true.

Once you have created your list of strengths, take a look at how they match up with those of your partner:

- What strengths do you both have?
- What are the strengths that you have that your partner doesn't?
- What strengths does your partner have that you don't have?
- How do your combined strengths balance each other out, conflict with one another, and/or overlap?

Now you're ready to start talking about the answers to the above questions, focusing on how you and your partner can combine your best traits in order to improve your relationship. The goal is to work together in a way that is cooperative, balanced, and keeps your partnership moving forward with strength and purpose.

WATCH YOUR WORDS

When you were a child, some adult in your life: a parent, teacher, or coach probably shared with you the old cliché, "Sticks and stones may break my bones but words can never hurt me." Millions of people have grown up hearing and believing this statement, probably even passing it along to their own children or grandchildren.

Here's the problem:
this saying is simply not true.

On the surface it seems okay because the intent is to remind us we shouldn't pay attention when others say unkind or untrue things about us. However, on a deeper level it's incredibly hard to ignore hurtful words because the truth is that words can (and do) have the power to hurt us.

Nowhere is this more apparent than with a partner relationship. Because partners know each other's vulnerabilities, sore spots, and "hot buttons" it's very easy to inflict painful wounds by making comments or statements directed at those tender areas. Chances are you have been the victim of this kind of wound at times in your life, and chances are you have also inflicted this kind of wound at times as well.

Because words can wound so deeply, they can also cause unnecessary battles to erupt over even the slightest issue. Think back over your relationship and you can almost certainly pinpoint a time when there were unkind words spoken, feelings were hurt, and an argument followed. The sad part is that most of the time these situations are both unnecessary and avoidable.

Before you say anything that may be hurtful, pause for a moment and ask yourself this question that I always ask myself: "Do the words I speak bring pleasure or pain?" The answer will make it obvious whether you should move forward with those words or opt for another, more respectful comment. It is much easier to not use hurtful words than it is to use them and then wish you could take them back.

NEVER USE SEX AS A WEAPON

This is a classic situation used by couples from those just starting out to those who have been together for many, many years. Why is using sex as a weapon so common? Because withholding sex can be a very powerful weapon for expressing anger, resentment, and general unhappiness to your partner. Sex is an integral part of any healthy relationship. It creates closeness, intimacy, and deep bonds of connection. It's a highly desirable activity, and so it becomes a very strong weapon when one partner chooses to withhold it from the other for any reason.

While withholding sex can be effective in the short run as a way to let your partner know you're angry, upset, or unhappy, the long term damage caused by using this strategy can be huge. It won't happen all at once, but over time, the more often sex is used as a weapon and withheld as a punishment, the more fragile and distant a relationship becomes.

There are many reasons why men and women both might choose to withhold sex as a "punishment" against their partner. You might be mad about something real or imagined your partner did, or perhaps you just want to put your partner in the stockades when you don't get your way. For some people, it's also a way to express jealousy or envy. In nearly every case, the underlying cause is that one or both partners are reluctant or afraid to talk about their problems or issue directly, instead they withold sex as a way to express their resentment without having to engage in an open, honest conversation.

Of course, declining to have sex is not always about hurting your partner. The reality of life is that men and women often have different levels of sex drive at different times, so when one partner is in the mood the other partner may not be. When this happens, it's important to talk respectfully and honestly with each other to communicate clearly and accurately about what is going on.

The reality of life is that your partner may have a different level of sex drive

Sometimes a pattern of mismatch between sexual desires has more to do with individual preferences and comfort zones. For instance, you might typically be "in the mood" in the evening, but your partner has the strongest desire in the morning. Talk about these and come up with a way to compromise so that both of you have opportunities to enjoy sex at a time when you are most likely to be interested. If you don't have this discussion, it's easy for you and your partner to each have misconceptions about what is happening and interpret the issue as sex being used as a weapon.

Another way that sex can become a hurtful weapon in a relationship is when you or your partner has doubts about sexual abilities, performance, or skill. Much of this is due to inaccurate portrayals of sex in the media, creating pressure to have the kind of sexual experiences that are just not real.

Talk with each other at a time when you are relaxed and comfortable to share information about what you like, what you don't like, and what you want more of in your sex life. This kind of open, honest, and intimate communication is a wonderful way to improve your sex life and it will create a stronger connection with your partner. It is the path to a deeper, more satisfying sexual life where both of your needs are met and fulfilled.

Ten More Building Blocks To Fortify Your Relationship Castle

We've touched on ten very helpful "building blocks" for strengthening and improving your relationship, but I have more to share with you. Read on for the next group of ten building blocks for enhancing your partnership!

CHECK YOUR BEHAVIOR

Sometimes when there are stresses or difficulties in a relationship, it is because one or both partners are not aware of how their own behavior is contributing to the problem. Even the smallest of details that seem insignificant to one partner can become extremely annoying and irritating to the other partner over time.

Start with the "big" behaviors: your tone of voice, the words you use, affection, attitude, communication, and so on. If none of these are the primary source of conflict, turn your attention to the smaller things in your daily interactions. Just as a very small rock can be very painful if it gets caught inside your shoe, your relationship can also suffer if the little annoyances are not confronted and resolved.

Here's a perfect example from my own marriage. My husband prefers that the toilet paper be refilled so that the toilet paper sheets will come out over the top of the roll. I thought that this was silly; after all, it shouldn't matter which direction it unrolls as long as there is still some on the roll to use! My response was to laugh it off and ignore his preference because I discounted the value of that preference. This was understandably irritating and annoying. He felt his preferences were dismissed and so he was hurt.

Once I realized just how important it was to him, I began making sure the toilet paper came off the roll from the top every single time. For me, it was a very small change to make in my habits, but for him it was an important thing. By acknowledging this and changing my behavior, he felt valued, appreciated, and loved. He still notices and says "thank you" for this little bit of extra effort I make on his behalf.

The really great thing is that we both are more aware of the impact and influence of small things (like hanging toilet paper) and show our caring and affection by doing these little things for each other whenever possible.

What about your relationship? I bet you can think of one or more of these little things. Why not do something about them sooner rather than later?

REPAIR AND BUILD

If your castle was damaged in a windstorm, I am sure you would make repairs as soon as possible. Perhaps the battlements lost some reinforcements, or maybe your main gate was blown over into the moat. Whatever it is, you understand it's important to fix it right away so it doesn't get worse or cause more problems down the road.

Most people don't stop to think about it, but the same concept applies to your relationship as well. When emotional damage occurs, if you ignore it and don't make repairs immediately the problem will only get worse and even more damage will result. Why does this happen? Why don't we make repairs to our relationship as promptly as we would make them to our house?

Because fixing emotional hurts can be hard. It's tough to talk about emotional hurts and damages because it's not always easy to discuss them calmly, honestly, and respectfully. When emotions run high the potential for conflict is even higher. How do you make the necessary repairs to your relationship and move forward in a positive way?

The first step is to acknowledge the hurts that have been afflicted, apologize and then forgive each other immediately. What's past is past, so leave it behind and start all over again. The next step is to talk about what caused the hurt in the first place. Be open and honest, sharing with your partner your feelings and what changes you would like him/her to make. As scary as this might seem, remember this: in most cases, your partner probably doesn't mean to hurt or offend you. They may not even realize what they said or did to cause it and will be anxious to correct it in the future. It is best to give them the benefit of the doubt and tell them so that it doesn't become a recurring painful torture.

A great way to help your partner recognize when words or behavior that create conflict and upset are occurring is to agree in advance on a subtle signal the two of you can share. When the signal is given, your partner realizes that what they are doing is hurtful or irritating and can stop right away. The signal can be a word, a gesture, or anything else the two of you agree on. It won't take very many times using the signal for his/her behaviors to change for the better.

My husband once told me that it really bothered him that I would regularly interrupt him when he was talking to someone or butt in with comments when he was telling a story to someone else. Being honest with myself, I knew that I did this but I hadn't thought it was a big deal; after all, I was just helping him to get the story straight or giving some left out facts. After I realized that it bothered him, I asked him to give me a signal, something other than stopping and saying "Hey! I'm telling the story!" We worked out that he would just clear his throat and I would realize that I had done it again.

Because I had been doing this for a very long time, it was a habit that I had to consciously monitor and be aware of until I developed a new habit of listening to his stories and keeping my version to myself. I have a saying "Fight only the fights that, in the long term, really need to be fought." I think this applies to this situation; I knew that in the long term my version of the stories wasn't going to change anything, and that it wasn't worth the bad feelings created from me butting in or my resulting hurt feelings when he would tell me to be quiet.

I appreciated that he would give me the signal rather than stopping me verbally in front of other people. We have come a long way, to the point where now he will even say, "Deb, do you have anything to add?" if he sees that I really want to say something.

The more you work on banishing the emotional hurts the easier the maintenance on your castle will be.

WE ALL NEED TO BE NEEDED

The mark of a healthy and balanced relationship castle is two partners who are secure enough in them-selves to be self-sufficient rather than being overly dependent on the other person. Sometimes, though, this self-sufficiency becomes so strong that the other partner does not feel needed. Everyone needs to be needed on some level, so if you want your relationship to flourish let your partner do things for you from time to time.

In my case, I used to think that asking my husband to do things for me meant I was somehow imposing on him, inconveniencing him, or that I wasn't doing my fair share. This feeling was so strong that I focused on being really self-sufficient so I wouldn't have to ask for help. Even when my husband offered to help by running an errand, going to the store, cleaning the house, or the like, I would always say "no thanks, I can do it" and then take care of it myself.

The impact of this behavior was noticeable. My husband came to feel that I didn't need him in any personal way, and that I was just fine without him. He felt left out and unwanted in many ways. On the other hand, I had taken on so many responsibilities and chores that I came to feel I was the only one giving anything to our relationship. I thought my husband didn't care about me and I grew resentful. This of course created conflict in our relationship and we went through a few months of tough going.

Once we started talking about what was happening and our feelings about it, I realized I had caused a lot of the problems by focusing on being so super self-sufficient. The more I shut him out and did things for myself, the more isolated from me he felt and the more resentful I became. We had some wonderful conversations together, and we both discovered the benefits of making sure we each felt needed by the other.

I found my husband was more than happy to help me and do things for me if I let him. I also found out there were things he wanted me to help with but was reluctant to ask because I overwhelmed by doing so much on my own. All in all, discussing this issue and doing things for each other have added a great deal of strength and intimacy to our relationship.

How does this show up in your relationship? Take an inventory of yourselves to be sure you aren't pushing each other away or blocking each other out. It helps to remember that everyone wants to feel needed and wanted, so make it a priority to give that gift to your partner.

BE DEPENDABLE

A strong relationship is one where you and your partner have grown to trust each other and depend on each other. Each of you knows that it's okay to count on the other because that person is dependable. You know you are the top priorities in each other's lives. You do what you say you will do and keep your commitments, no matter how small.

The message you communicate by being dependable is powerful and clear. It says I am not just someone passing through your life; I will always be there for you. It is an incredibly connected way of living that creates tremendous energy, love, and well being in your relationship.

Most people really want to be dependable. They think they can do this by saying "yes" whenever their partner asks them do something for them or be there for them. The problem with this approach is that they end up over-committing themselves and cannot fulfill all of their commitments. So what started out as an effort to be dependable turns into being undependable because they don't always get done what they said they would do.

The way to solve this problem is to be very careful about the commitments you make to your partner and others. It's perfectly okay to say "no." Saying no can be hard, especially for women, but once you get the hang of it you'll be amazed at how much easier it is to be a loving and dependable partner.

DO THE UNEXPECTED

Every relationship castle has to have a certain amount of routine. There are always walls to reinforce, towers to build, moats to dig, and stables to clean. However, every relationship castle also needs the surprise and fun of the unexpected every so often. You can do much to strengthen your relationship and make your partner feel appreciated by periodically doing something unexpected or unusual.

For instance, you might:

- Prepare a candlelight dinner
- Load the dishwasher without being asked
- Clean the house on Friday evening so your Saturday morning is free for doing something fun
- Mow the lawn when it's not your turn
- Wash and vacuum out your partner's car

- Make his/her favorite dessert
- Have ice cream sundaes for dinner
- Bring home flowers for no reason at all

My sister-in-law and I once told our husbands that we were taking them on a mystery date and to clear their calendar for those two days. When the time came, we packed for them, took them to the airport, and got on a plane to go to Universal Studios in Los Angeles. It was a blast, and they loved the surprise trip.

You'll find it pretty easy to think of unexpected things to do for your partner, and it can really be a lot of fun to put a plan in place. Be sure, though, to let your partner know you put in extra planning and effort especially for them.

This does not mean, though, you should be pushy about it or present it in a way that implies that your partner owes you something for your effort. The best way to handle it is when your partner says "thank you;" just say "you're welcome, I wanted to do something special for you."

When your partner does something unexpected for you, be sure to say "thank you" and let them know how much you appreciate their extra effort and thoughtfulness!

PATIENCE, PATIENCE, PATIENCE

Patience is a virtue, especially when it comes to your relationship. Even the best relationship has its ups and downs that require each partner to be patient, kind, thoughtful and patient some more. The more you practice loving patience with each other, the better and stronger your relationship castle will become.

Of course, it's not always effortless. In fact, it's often really hard. It's easy to become frustrated when your partner is doing something or saying something that irritates you or when they don't understand your needs. This is the time, though, when you have to be your most patient, repeating things as many times as it takes, speaking softly and kindly even when you want to let out a huge scream.

Know, that it's okay if at first your partner doesn't quit understand you, give it some time. Sometimes it takes longer than expected for your thinking to match up and coordinate. Keep talking it out and with patience, love, and mutual respect. The two of you will eventually come together in agreement. Throughout the process, be open to your partner's needs and offer encouragement and support as needed.

And above all else, practice your very best patience, patience, patience!

SPEAK KINDLY

In the last chapter we talked about the importance of choosing your words carefully so they don't hurt and aren't dismissive. Here we're going to take a slightly different approach and add on another consideration that can have a powerful impact on the way your words are received.

I'm talking about the way you speak, including your tone, inflections, speed, and volume. Pay attention to yourself, ensuring that you speak kindly, slowly, softly, and patiently. When talking to your partner who you love, keep your tone and volume calm and comfortable. It's easy to slip into a gruff, shrill, loud or biting tone of voice when you're feeling frustrated, which is then perceived by your partner as sounding angry, accusatory, hateful, or rude.

A raised voice or angry tone sounds to your partner like you are personally attacking them or accusing them of something. It can also say to them "I'm mad at you," "You're worthless to me," "I don't like you," or even "I wish you weren't here." Talking fast or impatiently can say to your partner "You're not important enough to take time for," "I think you're stupid," or "If I didn't have to talk to you it would be better." You can see that the way you use your voice makes a big difference in how your partner thinks you feel about them. It's worth the

> *A raised voice or angry tone sounds to your partner like you are personally attacking them*

few extra seconds it takes to take that extra breath, calm down, and then to say what it is you need to say in a way that is respectful and loving.

When you speak kindly to your partner, the message you communicate is much more likely to be heard and understood. Make sure the way you're speaking does not shift the focus away from what you are really trying to say. Speaking kindly allows your partner to pay closer attention to your words and your message.

GIVE AND ACCEPT

Placing blame is often the primary focus when there is a disagreement. "You did this..." and "You did that..." are common phrases couples use to accuse each other of a wide variety of misdeeds. This kind of blaming usually causes the argument to grow bigger and bigger, more rapidly than you might think possible. Partners then get so focused on "winning" the blame battle that they forget about the issue or problem that led to the argument in the first place.

Some adults don't recognize themselves doing this at all; they prefer to say they are standing up for themselves, defending their boundaries, or something similar. From the outside, though, watching two people lash out at each other with accusation and blame is just like watching two children in the schoolyard pointing fingers at each other when the teacher asks who started the fight. Back and forth they go; each intent on getting the other into trouble while avoiding any responsibility themselves.

When you find yourself in this kind of situation with your partner, make the choice to use the "give and accept" approach. It's a simple and straightforward way to prevent disagreements from escalating and helps the two of you resolve the issue at hand.

How does it work? You give the other person credit when they do something positive, no matter how small it might be, and accept some blame when the situation calls for it. This does not mean you should take on all the blame just to end the argument, but it does mean using the "give and accept" tool to work through disagreements.

Even when the issue really is not your fault, you can still help the situation by saying, "I'm sorry this happened" or "I'm sorry if I did something to hurt you or upset you." This opens up a dialogue where your partner can respond to you while still saving face and reducing damage to their pride or ego. The discussion can then move along in a productive way rather than turning into a sword fight of blame and accusations.

Remember, even if you are not at fault it's okay to say some version of "I'm sorry" to your partner. If you say "I'm sorry" it doesn't always mean you were wrong, just that you are sorry the situation has come to this difficult point. In my experience, this easy technique is a powerful way to get past placing blaming and get on with solving the issue at hand.

JOY AND PAIN

Life is full of joy and pain, sorrow and excitement, anticipation and fear, and so many other conflicting emotions that it can be really hard to deal with these experiences all alone. Most people find it much better and easier to lean on someone else for support and encouragement along the way. This is especially important when it comes to loving partners, because an integral part of having a strong and healthy relationship castle is sharing these experiences with each other.

We've talked before about putting your partner first in your life and giving first priority to fulfilling the wants and needs of your loved one. Now let's take this idea even deeper by focusing on how to grow closer to your partner by sharing in their dreams and feelings. Being together means not having to be alone, it's always having someone you trust and rely on close at hand.

Strengthen your relationship by sharing in your partner's dreams, joys, tears, hurts, and more. Lift them up when they feel weak or helpless, and encourage them when they feel discouraged or beaten down. Sharing your partner's joy and pain means loving them unconditionally especially when they feel worthless and helping them to see how precious they really are.

Never make fun of your partner. Never hurtfully tease them. Your job is to support and lift them up.

Be happy for your partner when something good happens to them, or when they are joyful. Show how proud you are when they succeed at something or do something that's really good that they are proud of. Be companionate when they are feeling hurt or are going through something that is difficult for them.

Be aware, though, that sharing in your partner's joy and pain does not mean taking on that pain as your own. It's not your burden to carry, and as much as you would like to spare your partner from the pain, you can't make it go away by putting it all upon your own shoulders. Offer support, encouragement, a shoulder to cry on, a quiet hug, or just a place to vent feelings and frustrations, but don't try to make things better by taking it all on yourself.

SUPPORTING DREAMS

Remember that putting someone else as "most important to you" also means offering full support for their dreams, passions, and life goals. In a loving committed relationship this is important because getting on board to support your partner's dream, project, goals, or job, is a powerful way of showing that your partner is a high priority in your life. This leads to stronger feelings, closer connections, and an improved sense of being together in a healthy partnership.

You partner's dreams may be as simple as a hobby they wish to pursue, taking a class, writing a book, or as major as a career shift. When you support your partner's dreams, you demonstrate how important they are to you. On the other hand, a lack of support can result in feelings of bitterness, worthlessness, disappointment and anger. Offering support does not mean you automatically want to do the same things as your partner does; it just means you are interested enough in your partner's happiness and well being that you commit yourself to providing the support and encouragement necessary for success.

So what do you do if your partner's dreams are too risky, unrealistic, or threatening to your financial or emotional security? This situation is a bit touchy or tricky, because you want to offer support but at the same time you cannot sacrifice those things which are critical to your financial or emotional security.

The best approach is to explore your partner's dreams in more detail, asking for information and determining exactly why this is so important to them. Most of the time you'll find it is some other entirely different issue or desire that's underlying the whole thing. After all, they wouldn't want to jeopardize those things either.

Once you have uncovered what the true motivation behind their dream, hobby or career change is it's much easier to plan a safe and effective path for them to accomplishing their goal.

Add Another Ten (Plus One Bonus) To Finish

As we approach the final chapter of building blocks for strengthening your relationship castle, remember that the ideas presented in this book are intended to help you and your partner improve the strength and quality of your relationship. Some ideas are better suited for your situation than others, so it's important that you both are comfortable applying the information I've provided and making adjustments as necessary for your particular circumstances.

And so we move into the last ten building blocks (plus one bonus) for your relationship castle!

ABOVE AND BEYOND

You probably had an experience in a bank, restaurant, or store where the person helping you went above and beyond the minimum effort necessary to meet your needs. This person wasn't satisfied with doing the minimum amount of work required; instead they took a real interest in your situation and committed themselves to finding the right solution no matter what.

While this kind of above and beyond approach is relatively common in our everyday dealings with other people, it is unfortunately not all that common in our most important personal relationships. I find it really interesting that we tend to treat our family, our partner, and those closest to us in ways that are far more unkind and disrespectful than we do those at work, at church, or even walking down the street. You would think it would be just the opposite, right?

In our family we raised our children with a saying that I continue to apply in my life to this day, "Treat family better than you treat company." It should be a very obvious thing to do, yet most people think they have the right to be hurtful or dismissive to loved ones simply because they can. I see parents doing this with their children a lot, and it really bothers me because it's so destructive and unnecessary.

For instance, I was in a restaurant when a child a few tables away spilled her milk. The mother responded right away by saying "That was stupid. Don't you know we'll have to pay for another glass of milk?" The child appeared to wilt before my very eyes, as you can well imagine.

How different the child would have felt if only her mother's response had been, "Oops! Don't worry, it was just an accident; we'll get it cleaned up." The child would have felt loved and supported instead of feeling defeated and put down. If the mother had stopped to think before reacting to the spilled milk, she could have asked herself "What would I say if this happened to a guest, an acquaintance or a friend?" The entire situation would have unfolded in a very different (and more positive) way.

I like to think of going above and beyond with loved ones as an act of charity. Charity is a special type of caring and support that's kind, selfless, giving, loving, being present, building up, protecting, and nurturing. It is never negative, discouraging, mean, childish, hurtful, or selfish.

Go above and beyond to treat your family better than you would anybody else!

The next time you find yourself in a situation such as this with a loved one or partner, make a conscious choice to pause for a moment and think about your response. Ask yourself what you would do if the person involved was a co-worker or friend rather than a close partner, and then take the right action. Go above and beyond to treat your family better than you would anybody else!

BUILD UP YOUR PARTNER

This one is similar to the previous building block, but takes a slightly different approach. It is based on the same concept, that we often treat friends and acquaintances better than we treat family, and looks at it from the perspective of how we can choose to build up or tear down our partner.

Of course the preferred action is to build up your partner, but what does this mean in the real world? Here are some examples to get you thinking:

- Don't put your partner down either privately or in public
- Always focus on the positive things about your partner
- Defend your partner if someone else says something negative or derogatory
- Don't say negative things about or to your partner, even in a joking way; it doesn't change anything to say, "Just kidding" when you're finished
- Joking about your partner can be hurtful, painful, and ultimately will create lasting damage to your relationship

Can you see the pattern emerging here? Life is hard enough as it is and full of times when your partner may feel discouraged, down, and even worthless. Don't add to it by tearing your partner down even further. Your responsibility as a loving committed partner is to build your partner up, giving him/her the confidence and encouragement necessary to keep moving forward in pursuit of a fulfilling life.

Before moving on to the next building block for your relationship castle let me emphasize something about building up your partner. It does not mean to give false flattery, misleading praise, or otherwise lie to your partner just to make them feel good. This is the worst kind of treatment you can give, setting them up for failure with false information. Telling a spouse that his green tie goes with his blue shirt, when it is a definite clash, is not helpful. Although it may be hard sometimes to speak a difficult truth directly to your partner's face, in the long run it is much better to face the issue and be honest than to sidestep the issue and be misleading. Give honest positive compliments and information that will help them and build them up so that when they receive outside comments from peers they will receive the same input.

ENERGY = COMMON VISION

A common trait of relationships that are vibrant, healthy, and strong is the intense energy that is created when the partners share a common vision and purpose. You may have heard the phrase "the whole is greater than the sum of its parts." It applies here. A solid partnership where the couple shares a common purpose and a common vision will be filled with a rich and powerful energy that will bring them together into something much larger than just the two individuals.

How do you go about creating this kind of energy fuelled by a common vision? It's all about bringing positive energy and feelings into the relationship, being certain that personal interactions between partners will create closer connections, stronger bonds, and more fulfilling results. This may sound difficult to achieve, but it is really very easy when you know the right way to go about it.

If this is the kind of partnership you want, then make it a habit to always think in positive terms, all the time and no matter what is going on around you. Keep negative thoughts, feelings, and actions out of your relationship, and make it a top priority to work together in unity.

I heard that there was a sign in the locker room of the NFL's New England Patriots that says, "Individuals play the game, but teams win championships." This applies just as strongly to partners and relationships as it does to a professional football team.

DATING – FUN AND UNIQUE

When you and your partner first began dating, it was probably a time of wonder, joy, and intense feelings. The two of you really wanted to be together just for the sheer pleasure of it, and over time you came to rely more and more on each other's companionship, encouragement, and support. Those were good times, weren't they? It seemed possible back then and you looked forward to a long and happy life together in your castle as King and Queen of your kingdom.

So what happened? Where did all of those warm, happy, and pleasant feelings go? Somewhere along the way, real life intruded into the fairy tale and the realities of being together day in, day out, took over. As time went by, especially if children came into the picture, there were fewer and fewer moments when the two of you could just be together. There were chores to do, careers to build, children to care for, and much more. So by the time you took care of all those responsibilities you had little (if any) energy left for each other. Add into all that the inevitable disagreements and conflicts and the picture gets even bleaker.

Does this sound familiar? If so, you're definitely not alone. Even the best and strongest relationships go through periods when life gets overwhelming and partners start to drift apart. The great news, though, is that fixing this problem is easy. It takes some time and some consistent commitment, but you will start seeing results very quickly. And even more importantly, it's fun!

The idea here is to repair and rebuild your relationship by committing your valuable time to the process.

The answer is to start dating again. Just as you did when you were first getting to know each other, schedule time at least once a week (or more, if possible) when the two of you set aside everything else and go on a date. You can schedule time in the evening, on a weekend day, or even at lunchtime during the work week. It doesn't have to be fancy, nor expensive, and it doesn't have to take up several hours. The idea here is to repair and rebuild your relationship by committing your valuable time to the process.

My husband and I have done this for many years, and it has been a huge part of how we stay connected with each other. We used to have an arrangement that we would spend every Friday together, and took turns making arrangements for the date. The planner would tell the other person what to wear, what time to be ready, and that was about it; everything else was a surprise until we actually set out on the date.

The interesting thing is that as much as we benefited from regular time together, we benefited almost as much from the process of planning the date. It was a whole lot of fun coming up with new ideas, putting plans together, and then surprising each other with the details. Because of this, we did things that we would not have done otherwise. What kind of things? Here are just a few examples:

- We went to a body building championship
- We went to a horse pulling competition
- We went flying in a plane over our house
- We went dancing at a place we had never been
- We ate in small out-of-the-way places
- We went hiking, bowling, and motorcycle riding
- We went to the county fair
- We packed a picnic and watched a dog Frisbee catching contest in the park
- We went to the local feed store to see baby animals

- We took a wagon ride out in the snow to see elk being fed
- We rented snowmobiles
- We went to the local Parade of Homes event
- We sat in the hot tub and gazed at the stars
- We went fishing on free fishing day
- We went to sporting events at the university and high school, such as football, basketball, volleyball, and soccer
- We went to a hockey game (it was my first, and ever since I've been hooked on the sport!)

Whew! That's a pretty long list, and it doesn't begin to capture the amazing range of activities we have enjoyed on our dates. Now, some of the things we've done did cost money, but many more of them have been free or nearly free. In fact, some of the very best dates were the ones when it took creativity and imagination to put together a low or no cost date! The possibilities are limitless, and what you gain from the process is far more than you invest in it.

Still not quite sure? Here are a few more ideas from my friends, family, and past experience:

- Attend a cowboy poetry reading
- Attend a business seminar
- Enjoy a free concert in the park
- Go to the circus
- Tour a local factory
- Play tennis
- Play racquetball
- Fly kites
- Go swimming

- Go out for ice cream
- Take a dance class
- Learn how to knit
- Carve pumpkins on Halloween
- Play card games
- Paint pictures
- Take a cooking class
- Enter a snow sculpting contest
- Go sledding
- Go kayaking
- Walk along a path holding hands
- Volunteer at a local charity event
- Lie on a blanket and look for shapes in the clouds
- Go to the garden store and enjoy looking at the spring flowers
- Sit on top of a hill and watch the sunset

Remember, you don't need to spend a lot of money -- just use your imagination. Have fun and experience new things; don't just go to the movies or watch TV together for every date. Think of it as a great way to get out and experience more of life by getting away on a mini "vacation" each week.

Now it's your turn. What terrific date ideas can you come up with?

THE 3 C'S

It's easy to get caught up in your daily activities, putting your focus on getting everything done. This usually involves dividing up the responsibilities, with each partner taking on a share of the load. It's a very efficient way of doing things, but it is also an easy way to fall into the bad habit of taking each other for granted. Before long, the two of you lose sight of the little things that you love about each other; the kinds of things that make you laugh, smile, or feel all warm and fuzzy inside.

The remedy for this is to compliment your partner at least three times each day. I call these my 3 C's. They must be sincere compliments, not just passing comments that are shallow and automatic. When you give compliments, focus in on your partner and notice the things that are simple, yet special. Here are some examples of the kind of compliments I give my husband each day:

- *I like how you make me smile*
- *I love that you are dependable*
- *You look great in that blue shirt*
- *It's fun to be around you*
- *I appreciate when you rub my back*
- *I feel safe with you*
- *I love going places with you*

Another variation on this is to express gratitude for something your partner has said or done, no matter how small it may seem. Some examples of this include:

- *Thank you for taking me out to dinner*
- *Thank you for being so nice to me*
- *Thank you for being so brave and strong when I'm afraid*
- *Thank you for working so hard for our family*

- *Thank you for doing the dishes*
- *Thank you for holding the door open*
- *Thank you for the loving hug*

The bottom line is that practicing the 3 C's faithfully will make both of you feel better about yourselves and each other. It might seem a little uncomfortable or strange at first, but once you discover how happy it makes both you and your partner it will quickly become easy, natural, and a prized habit.

LISTEN WITH YOUR EYES AND EARS

I have talked about the importance of honest communication between partners, including kind words and showing respect. There is another part of communication, though, that is less commonly talked about but makes up over 85% of the messages we send and receive. These are the nonverbal cues of communication, such as body position, eye contact, movement, gestures, tone of voice, and facial expressions. These communication elements are incredibly important, and often reveal a person's true thoughts, feelings, and concerns more clearly than their words alone.

When you talk with your partner, listen with both your eyes and your ears. By paying attention to non-verbal cues as well as the spoken word you can get a more complete understanding of what your partner is really trying to communicate. Here are some of the things to watch:

- **Eye contact** – When your partner holds steady eye contact it shows confidence, and calm. If they look away, look down, or avoid eye contact it shows they are uncomfortable, nervousness, that they may be holding something back or are being deceitful.

- **Movement** – If your partner shifts their weight back and forth, continually changes position in a chair or backs away they are probably anxious, uncomfortable, and feel a desire to "get away." On the other hand if they stand still, sit calmly, or do not move away from you they are most likely confident, interested, and comfortable.

- **Tone of voice** – Speaking in a whispery tone of voice that is hard to hear shows shyness or nervousness. Speaking in a shrill, loud or exaggerated tone can show anxiety, lack of confidence, anger, or defensiveness.

- **Gestures** – Use of fast or exaggerated hand movements might show excitement, anger, nervousness or exaggeration. Limited hand movement shows confidence, comfort, and interest. Worry, anxiety, or boredom can be exhibited by no hand movement.

- **Face** – If their face is relaxed and they are smiling with open bright eyes it shows they are confident, comfortable, and happy. Watch for trembling lips or chin, closed eyes, teary eyes, or total lack of facial expression these show emotions of sadness, fear, upset, nervousness or unhappiness.

If your partner's body language shows something is not quite right, gently encourage him/her to let their thoughts and feelings come out. Ask them to open up and then be patient; it may take some time, gentle touches, and a few false starts for them to let the real information to come out.

Try not to interrupt, correct, or jump in and offer solutions right away. Let your partner talk at a pace that they find comfortable and safe. While they talk you need to focus your attention 100% on them and their needs. The simple act of being attentive to your partner creates a strong sense of caring, comfort, and love.

CREATING MORE AFFECTION

When partners start to drift apart, get distracted by outside things, or otherwise divert themselves from being fully present in the relationship, one of the first noticeable results is a reduction in affection. They may stop holding hands, kiss less often, avoid hugs, and sometimes go as far as to avoid making love. It's another one of those vicious cycles that gets worse and worse. Disconnection leads to less affection, less affection leads to disconnection, and so on.

The great news, though, is that you can reverse this cycle easily just by making new choices to bring more affection into your relationship. Make a point of holding hands, walking arm in arm, and giving appropriate hugs and kisses in public. This doesn't mean having a major "make out" session in the food court at the mall and embarrassing other people, but it does mean reaching out and making physical contact with your partner consistently. At first you might have to make a conscious effort to do this, but very quickly it will become automatic because it feels so good.

You can take things further by making your hugs and kisses a bit longer. Try holding your hugs 10 seconds or even 20 seconds at a time. Why? Because it can take that long to fully create a good physical connection. Relax and breathe in the scent of your partner. Share the warm feelings this creates in you. Touch each other gently with a loving caress, not a brisk slap on the shoulder or back. Don't try to have a conversation with each other, just soak up the connection and enjoy a sweet affectionate hug.

The more affection between partners, the closer their emotional connection...

Now, going back to the cycle I talked about before, just as lack of affection feeds upon itself, so too does affection. The more affection between partners, the closer their emotional connection and the closer the emotional connection the more affection they will enjoy.

If your relationship could use a little more affection, you can make it happen quickly and easily just by choosing to be more affectionate on a regular basis!

A TEAM

A common reason relationships suffer is that the two partners don't work together as a team. Instead, they live and act as two separate people, each focusing the highest priority on themselves and what they want in life. This is a seriously destructive relationship attitude, and often leads to severely strained and even broken relationships.

How does it feel in your relationship? Do you and your partner work together and cooperate with each other as a team? If not, here are some things you can do to improve your partnership and come together as a strong, connected, and healthy team:

- Support each other in everything you can.

- Frequently do things together, from running errands to cleaning the house

- Create and set goals together as a team; you can have individual goals as well, but they should be consistent with your overall goals as a couple

- Make decisions together and be united when following up on those decisions

- Present a united front to children, family, and friends; when you have a disagreement, discuss and resolve it in private rather than putting the drama out there for everyone to see

- If you do or say something that is contrary to teamwork, acknowledge it, apologize to your partner, and move forward together

If you have any doubt about the critical importance of being together as a strong team, think about how a team operates in the world of sports. When things aren't going well the team members don't quit, they focus on coming together and working together even more. Each team member pitches in and gives 100% effort to the team goals. There's no hesitation, no waiting around, no blaming other players, just a lot of hard work and dedication to team success.

Your relationship should operate in the same way. Don't quit or give up on your partner, but instead focus on coming together and working together consistently. I always say "love without condition," so don't hold anything back; don't wait to see what your partner is going to do for you, reach out and do something for your partner. Don't wait to see if your partner is going to say "I love you," but instead open up and say, "I love you" to your partner first.

...working together as a team means loving each other no matter what.

You see, working together as a team means loving each other no matter what. It's easy to get lost in negative thoughts and then actually talk yourself right out of love, so don't give in to this common trap. Focus on caring for your partner rather than waiting to see how much your partner is going to care for you.

There's one more critical element to working as a team: God. Partnerships thrive best and remain strongest when God is included as an integral part of the team. Take turns saying a prayer together daily, and frequently give prayers of thanks and gratitude. Listen to what your partner is grateful for and what your partner thinks is important to pray for. Take a few moments after your prayers to meditate and reflect on what you have prayed for and how that figures into your lives. Make God a part of your team. With God's grace and guidance your castle will become impenetrable!

NEVER SAY "........."

These simple words should be stricken from your relationship vocabulary:

"You Never...." and *"You Always...."*

These may seem like simple or innocent words, but they are among the most destructive and hurtful ones to use with your partner. Why? Because the message they send is that you are never happy with your partner, your partner can never live up to your expectations, and your partner has a constant record of failure. The problem is that this is just not true.

No matter how bad things get or how unhappy you are with your partner, you're lying to yourself if you think your partner has "never" or "always" been a certain way. If this were true then you would not have become partners in the first place because there would have been no reason to be together.

When the words "never" and "always" enter into your conversations what you are doing is dismissing and discounting who your partner is and what your partner represents. It is the ultimate betrayal of your relationship and the time you have spent together.

It's no wonder these phrases cause so much pain and unhappiness in relationships!

So get rid of them. Right now. Banish them from your vocabulary forever.

LAUGH THROUGH IT

Of course you've heard the old saying "laughter is the best medicine," but you may not have heard the closely-related corollary to this classic bit of wisdom by Bill Cosby:

"If you can laugh at it, you can live through it."

Put simply, laughter makes you feel good, while laughing together with your partner makes you both feel good. It brings you closer and strengthens the bond and connection you have with each other. In fact, research shows that when you laugh together you are more attracted to each other. Sharing a good laugh has a way of putting life into perspective, it also allows you to let go of distractions and embrace being fully present in your relationship.

Laughing together is easy during good times, when everything in life is moving along happily and smoothly. What's harder is to laugh together when life isn't so great and your relationship is stressed or strained but this is exactly the time when you need laughter the most. I'm not talking about laughing "at" your partner or making fun of them in a way that is demeaning. Genuine laughter "with" each other reduces tension and re-focuses your attention on what's really important.

When you laugh together you forget all the reasons why you're mad at each other. By doing this you get a fresh perspective on the problems you're coping with at the moment. I find laughing together with my husband is almost a magical thing. We let go of resentments and conflicts, lean forward and focus on each other. Best of all we usually end up in a sweet, affectionate kiss.

ALL IN

 This is an easy concept but can feel really scary when it comes down to putting it into action in the real world. It's all about commitment, honesty, and giving yourself unconditionally. No matter the circumstance, no matter the issue or problem, your commitment to your partner is sure, unquestioned and unbending. It brings together the concepts, ideas and building blocks I've discussed throughout this book, closing the loop to complete the strengthening of your relationship castle.

You see, a relationship only works if you jump in with both feet. You can't be "part in" and "part out" at the same time. Holding back and waiting to see if things get better on their own, before committing your own attention and energy to the situation just doesn't work. This is why so many people drift through life, never quite connecting with another person and never quite letting anyone into their heart enough to experience the magic of a loving, healthy, and committed relationship.

Think about the first time you climbed up onto the high dive at the local pool so you could jump off into the water. It seemed like a good idea when you were firmly down on the ground, but from the perspective of being up on the high dive it seemed pretty scary and maybe not the best idea after all. You could stay up there, waffling back and forth about whether to jump, or you could set aside your fears and jump, trusting everything will be okay and you would soon feel great about yourself. In other words, you chose to be "all in" on the high dive. The same thing holds true right now in your relationship – choose to be "all in" and you'll soon feel great about both yourself and your partner.

Choose to be "all in" and you'll soon feel great about both yourself and your partner.

It's easy to get caught up in trying to explain why you avoid being all in, but this is pretty much a waste of time and energy. Instead of looking back, choose to look forward and choose to be committed to your partner. This means talking through problems at the first sign of conflict, working on those problems from a perspective of love and respect, and focusing on truly understanding the needs of your partner.

There's no holding back emotionally, physically, or intellectually. Do whatever it takes to make them feel valued and loved so your relationship endures and grows in strength and power through the years.

So set aside your fears, focus on the future, and jump in enthusiastically with both feet. Congratulations, you've made the choice to be "all in!"

Final Thoughts

Here we are at the end of the book. I sincerely hope you have already started to implement the information presented here. It is all from the real world and can absolutely help you create dramatic changes in your relationship, but ultimately it is up to you and your partner to make the necessary changes. Before bringing this to a close, there are a few final thoughts I'd like to share with you.

A JOURNEY, NOT A DESTINATION

It's easy to fall into the trap of thinking that once you resolve a problem with your partner you can live happily ever after. After all, you can fix a broken door and expect it to stay fixed for a long time, right?

Unfortunately, relationships are not as simple or stationary as a door in your castle. They are ever changing and continually in motion. What's more, the way you and your partner interact and approach your relationship has a powerful direct influence on the direction and intensity of its motion.

Here's another example to consider. Did you know that the Golden Gate Bridge is constantly being painted? Workers start painting on one end and work their way to the other end. As soon as they're finished, they go back to where they started and do it all again.

If they didn't follow this continuous maintenance routine, the bridge would soon start to deteriorate and weaken. The elements of the harsh ocean are constantly inflicting damage on the bridge, so the maintenance people have to continuously protect the bridge with fresh paint to prevent any damage.

Relationships are exactly the same; just as workers are constantly painting the Golden Gate Bridge, a relationship is a continual work in progress. You, as partners must continually protect it from the harsh environment of the real world. If you think you have the perfect relationship right now and choose to never work at it again, I guarantee you it will die.

Love needs constant nourishment to flourish. When you and your partner continually work together to keep your relationship healthy, it grows very deep roots that nourish and support your love more and more each day. Most couples find it easy to pay attention to their relationship when it's new and fresh, but over time they gradually get distracted by other things and their attention wanders elsewhere. This is when a relationship can start to take a back seat and therefore starts to deteriorate.

Love needs constant nourishment to flourish.

Always think of your relationship as a journey, not a destination. Keep working together consistently, paying as much attention to each other's needs as you did when you first began dating.

WHEN THINGS GET TOUGH, REMEMBER

No matter how often or how well you work on strengthening your relationship, there will be times when the going is very tough. You will probably even question the relationship itself at some point. It is at these times especially when you must be commited even more fully to your partner and truly be "all in" with your heart and soul.

When tough times occur, there are a number of things you can do that will keep you commited to the relationship and focus in on making repairs. Some examples include:

- Make a list of what caused you to fall in love with your partner
- Write down the qualities in your partner that you most appreciate and admire
- Think about why you are attracted to your partner
- Remember the things your partner does that make you feel good about yourself
- Think about how the things your partner does makes you feel about him/her
- Remind yourself each day of at least three things you love about your partner

- Think of at least one thing you can do to make your partner feel happy today

I won't sugar coat this by telling you these things are always easy. On the contrary, sometimes they can be very difficult indeed, especially when you are feeling angry, disappointed or resentful toward. I promise you, though, if you do these things with an open heart and with your full devotion the result will amaze you.

The result, you see, will be that you talk yourself back into love with your partner. Most people don't realize they have this power. Many times they focus on the negative things about their partner instead and talk themselves out of love, but you can change everything if you work instead on talking yourself into love. Take time to think about your partner and tell yourself you can't wait to be with them.

Each of you will progress through or handle issues at a different pace and in a different way. Allow your partner the time and patience necessary, because you can't expect or require more from your partner than they are able to give at that time.

Spend time everyday in positive self talk, thought, and proactive action. Your relationship will grow or decay in the same way that you are thinking, talking and acting. Have patience and understanding. Always remember....

"Nobody is perfect;
they only have perfect moments."

CASTLE OF YOUR DREAMS

By now I hope you realize just how strongly I believe in the ideas presented here. They have all been part of my marriage and relationship experience in some way, so be assured I have firsthand knowledge of the powerful impact they have. I am confident that with the implementation of this information it will improve your relationship as tremendously as it has improved mine.

I'll leave you with this final reminder: make your partner the highest and first priority in your life and your relationship will bloom no matter the season or situation the castle gardens are in.

More Famous Quotes by Debbie Gerber

- *"Marriage should be an "all in" activity - like skydiving. Once you make the commitment there is no going back."*

- *"In its very best and most noble moments, a healthy relationship is nothing short of magical."*

- *"Become the best partner you can be, focus your energy on doing everything necessary to be an engaged, interested and committed partner."*

- *"You have the power to change things by putting in the time and effort necessary to do your part to be the best partner you can possibly be."*

- *"If there is trouble in paradise and the alarm goes off don't hit the snooze button. You may be too late when you finally wake up."*

- *"The best way to have a great marriage is to create a great marriage."*

- *"Are you the kind of spouse that you would want to be married to?"*

- *"Give your partner the GIFT of the benefit of the doubt."*

- *"Love is like having an umbrella in a rain storm."*

- *"A strong relationship will be deep, connected, and fulfilling to your heart and soul."*

- *"Treat your spouse as if you were courting your favorite celebrity and you will feel like a celebrity."*
- *"Respecting your spouse sometimes means modifying your behavior."*
- *"Selfishness is the knife that cuts out the heart of love."*
- *"Love is giving the gift of you with no expectation of reciprocation."*
- *"A hug lasts long after the arms are removed."*
- *"Turn your marriage vows of "I Do" into "We will do it."*
- *"Make your spouse your top priority; know them well enough to fulfill their emotional needs and wants."*
- *"Your tone of voice is more powerful than what you say. A raised, frustrated or angry voice carries accusation in it."*
- *"Have you fulfilled the fine print of your marriage contract? The fine print was the expectations and dreams."*
- *"A successful marriage happens when you give your spouse what is important to them even if you don't understand it."*
- *"Affection creates more affection."*
- *"Love is to listen with your ears, observe with your eyes, understand with your heart, and show with your actions."*

ONLINE MARRIAGE IMPROVEMENT PROGRAM

Attaining Marriage Happiness In 7 Easy Steps

Act Now and Transform your current marriage into the Shining Castle on the hill where you are the King and Queen of your truly Happy and Fulfilling Marriage!

Please get this system now to get the answers and solutions to these questions and more.

- How do you stop teasing and put-downs in your marriage?

- Do you feel taken advantage of?

- How do you add fun and excitement to a marriage?

- Do you want your spouse to listen to you?

- Do you want compliments instead of criticism?

- What are the easy steps to rekindle the flame?

- Can the fighting and disappointment be stopped?

- Are you tired of being dumped on and run over?

- Are you getting what you want out of your marriage?

This online program is a complete step-by-step relationship refresher program. It gives you downloadable audios, videos and PDFs. Every couple should enjoy this journey of discovery for improving their marriage and adding fun and excitement to their relationship. Join today at:

http://www.relationshipcastlesystems.com

Dear Readers,

I love hearing about your experiences after putting the 31 Relationship Building Blocks into action. My mission is to improve my readers' lives, so nothing is sweeter than hearing about your accomplishments.

Email me at debj@scattergenius.com

Please join with me in *The Happy Marriage Crusade* today. I am excited to hear from you. Although I may not be able to answer all your emails personally your experience or story from your email may be in my next blog post, teleconference, video or book.

Visit the website and see.

Debbie

http://www.relationshipcastlesystems.com